The Art *of* Gravity

The Art *of* Gravity

POEMS

Jay Rogoff

LOUISIANA STATE UNIVERSITY PRESS   BATON ROUGE

Published by Louisiana State University Press
Copyright © 2011 by Jay Rogoff
All rights reserved
Manufactured in the United States of America
LSU Press Paperback Original

Designer: Laura Roubique Gleason
Typeface: Arno Pro

LIBRARY OF CONGRESS CATALOGING-IN-PUBLICATION DATA

Rogoff, Jay.
 The art of gravity : poems / Jay Rogoff.
  p. cm.
 ISBN 978-0-8071-3890-8 (pbk. : alk. paper) — ISBN 978-0-8071-3892-2 (epub) —
ISBN 978-0-8071-3891-5 (pdf.) — ISBN 978-0-8071-3893-9 (mobi)
 I. Title.
 PS3568.O486A89 2011
 811'.54—dc22
                    2011007641

To George Balanchine,
        Edgar Degas, and
                Suzanne Farrell,
                        dance geniuses,
and to Penny, my partner

Contents

The Art *of* Gravity

Invocation

Apollo! Onstage I stood
in leotard
and slippers, white tunic knotted
    at my shoulder, and I *knew,*
        like lecturing on quantum mechanics
        or batting, bases full, against Koufax,
    here I was, in trouble again. Apollo!

Oh dreams, fraught
    with inadequacy—
can't I impersonate
    a god in the privacy
        of my unconscious,
        dance
under cover of tactful night
    in a dark house,
        with no fear
        of a true mirror?
    Elusive muse!
    Then at my elbow Mr. B

(ten years dead)
materialized. I said,
    "I've never danced—"
        (at *all,* I meant)—
        My dear,
    he interrupted, his accent
        purring in my ear,
        you
are god
    of muses. You see danced
        ballet
        how many times? You know.

Thus bemused,
thus blessed,
    I (who'd never
        danced), I was Apollo,

set for the strains
of Stravinsky's score
to course like ichor
through my veins.
The curtain rose; I woke in the darkest
hour and never knew
what immortal long-legged darling he
(in conspiracy
with night) had cast:

my Terpsichore.

1   *The Code of Terpsichore*

Dancing is an action, showing outwardly the spiritual movements which must agree with those measures and perfect concords of harmony which, through our hearing and with earthly joy, descend into one intellect, there to produce sweet movements which, being thus imprisoned, as it were, in defiance of nature, endeavor to escape and reveal themselves through movement.

    —Guglielmo Ebreo da Pesaro, *On the Practice or Art of Dancing* (1463)

To know how to dance is to know how to control yourself.

    —Motto of the Gordon Dancing Academy in *Swing Time*

Museum

Quick sidelong glances
      clodhoppers in fourth position
          and you know
      this young woman
              you're trying to conceal you're studying studying
          with you this Degas
dancer dances
      so it's difficult not to imagine
            as you watch those flinging
            painted limbs the flinging

in precise abandon of these legs growing
      out of her clunky
          shoes like saplings springing
          from the pavement and inclining
             their two trunks
      like lovers toward each other irrevocably
            seeking a crux
and disappearing
                into the short
                shade of her black skirt.
                Art

is exciting. As you peek
      from the paint to the paint
          on her eyelids an identical
      mauve under Degas's light
and this, she shoots a look
          too quick to be meaningful
      and you've stopped breathing right
          so you haul
your attention back to the work
of art from the work

of art. Yes.
Yes the forms. This
      should be a decent

enough interval but when you look she's gone
so you turn
to see her walking, turned out
out
into the next gallery.
Hurrying to the center of the room you yearn
to raise
your hand *ah despair* but that
seems silly

so from afar you watch her thick-soled slenderness assume
second position in front of—
does it matter? The dance
must go on, her exit, your entrance
this absurd chasing from room to room
of art that must insist on inspiring
you and give
you nothing, nothing! you! savoring
this fruit-
less pursuit.

Latin Class

Herschel will be pissed
I know. We missed
last week and have practiced
      exactly once even
      after I cobbled some Van
      Dyke Parks and Steely Dan
          into a fake merengue tape.
          In a panic I tell you it's hope-
less but your Presbyterian genes insist
             so we try to look invisible
          among the couples trip-
             ping over each other in the high school
             gym and shrug when Herschel's cool
             skeptical
      eye stares us down.
He seizes Christy his partner by the wrist
          and they whip
             around each other in an impossible
          new step
      hips driving like some insane
      Caribbean machine
          and the others' jaws drop
             yeah right so I can tell we're all on an equal
                Anglo footing. We walk it through
                fast way too
          fast he cues the tape
             and suddenly it's carnival
      for spastics screaming out for correction
                Fellas! Fellas! oh
the wrist
          this way the hip
          that and now I'm not step-
             ping on your feet and the planetary whirl
      and shift of weight and tension
             in our arms feel
      fine
                    as I catch
          you in the orbital

                                                swing and watch
                    your eyes light up Caribbean
                                while Herschel
                                                bails out of our lurch-
                                ing path his smile
                    I imagine
barely suppressed
                    at us the Dominican champion
                            estrellas orientales as we dip
dangerously only to rise up in the East.

Umbrella Pines

Not chaste and balletic,
        Italy,
        but wildly wickedly
operatic:
                the umbrella pines
                won't dance
                        no matter
                                how their foliage might suggest
                        the gauze flutter
                of dancers' skirts, their slender trunks
                                resemble legs at rest.

But between the trunks light like Bellini's
        moves
in airy trapezoids, however the breeze
        contrives
as if the supple trees
                stepped
                once then stopped

to loom
        in splendor
                unreachable. Beneath
                we breathe
                        a hot voiceless
                                balsamic
                                music
                                        pregnant
        with pine and ranker
perfume
                                        whose descent
                        from those skirts along those limbs carries
        rich air
                                        dancing so as to haunt
        us in the sleepy heat and render
                                us faint
with arias of aroma.

Primavera

for Siobhan, Richard, and Deirdre Dunham

So what if love is carnality
      crossdressing as *caritas*?
      In spring sex goes
           dancing spinning at the center
              of a universe
phoney as Ptolemy
     in which we refuse
     to disbelieve. The metamorphosis
     of a goddess
         I mean a dancer
         into a mother
displaces
         her capacity for air
with roundness
            formerly a curse.
              Borne
              a thousand brilliant nights flown
        across the stage in the finale of *The Four*
Temperaments she would pose
             in open
        fourth forever
as in holy
                 conversation.
           Now with earth she shares
stranger energy
        with the moon peculiar
        humors
      a flush of radiance compared with which hot ballerinas
embody
equanimity.
      Not bulimia but morning sickness:
      how can she dance Chloris?
                purge
      her blood of thorns and roses
              to emerge
         as grace and nurse
                as Flora?

                        bear
             up under human changes
                        under
indignity
                                        this sleekest swiftest vessel taking on
                        the world's water
             pushing hard on the equinox
                                                devouring the entire spring
                                                        to bear a
                        daughter?

The ballet's grace
             clothes desire
                        barely
diaphanous
gown charitably tumbling about the voluptuous
             figure
                                        beguiling
                                        revealing.
                                                Light
springs from among dark aromatic trees
whose oranges
                                        participate
in the adoration of artifice.
                        Say those three
                                girls circling
             tentatively in their
                                                dance
are goddesses—
                        why argue?
             Even the spear-carrier
can disperse
             the clouds and augur weather
                                                fit for an entrance.

Let her find welcome in the natural
             air and in the scent of fruit
             and let her delight

in people and their sidereal
    motions and appetite.
            Let her bear no gravity no sorrow
                    and let her discard
                discord
                        like a worn
            pummeled dancing shoe.
        May the concrete
                            on which her first steps
stumble
turn floral
            meadow
a mortal
                        path strewn
        with the lucky shards of art.
                                May faithful music
                        dog her steps
making them graceful
                            making them rhythmic
making them above all
            suffice for transportation.

Turnout

Hovering, there, her precise arms,
        caressed by waves of blue stage light,
loom streamlined and supple as the pastel limbs
        of dancers Degas turned out,
        snapping off pirouette on pirouette,

his weird mauves and gaslit greens
        insinuating art turns out dancers
as workers turn out gorgeous, fast machines.
        Spectacularly her tutu flares
        under unnatural color that blurs

a face calm as a dolphin's. Her splayed
        feet, spread arms, mark her body's turn-
out, coaxed-open thighs and ribcage, so broad
        a smile that from the balcony no one
        reads strain under industrious sleek skin—

steel sinews, attent tendons, turned out
        on the axis of a lathe, each bone
stark as a cathedral rib, to strut
in magnanimous turnout this taut,
        relentlessly taught machine.

Yellow Dancers

Les Demoiselles four years before Picasso!
Their bestial, blank-as-canvas ritual masks,
question marks or quizzical asterisks
footnoting no point other than a toe shoe,
float featureless and fierce above the yellow
firestorms of their tutus. But not a sphinx
among them—they're vague girls, not odalisques
or oracles, not *matres dolorosae*.
Only the slipper-screaks and lewd skirt-whispers
cover the pumping, an occult explosion
driving their piston legs to such a heat
as resurrects love rising in the foot
(not eyes, not lips), the genius of an engine
igniting these parts to engender dancers.

Degas's Men

Degas's stage shows such a kingdom of women
you realize in the 1870s
the Opéra Ballet employed not one
danseur noble, no cavaliers, no hunks
to partner nymphs, lift sylphs, provide the muscle.
No; in Degas's world women reign, and we
study them closely, whether on pointe on
those custom-ordained legs, or curtsying
deeply to grant us a gaslit audience
with a breathless bodice, or backstage bending
their long forms over to adjust a slipper,
or hitching up a stocking or shoulder strap.
The orchestra have seen it all before:
legs, legs, legs, and anyway too busy
to adore, Delibes and Chabrier to tootle,
prodding the dancers with tall, deep bassoons.
Yet it's paradise, with perspiration
(can a dancer earn a living wage?),
these young limbs twining round these limbs of air,
this rustling kingdom of tulle growing fragrant.
Even the dark ministers loitering
in wings, rehearsal parlors, dressing rooms,
glimpsed in ill-lit corners, their obscure faces
inspecting legs and bodices, the two-
dimensional men like sinister cartoons,
matte black in a rounded world of pink satin
dyed blue and green by the infernal gaslight—
the fat, top-hatted Lucifers prepared
to tender hotel suites to couch these sweaty
angels, subscribing to weary loveliness
and gorging on it, waiting to assist
maman in snatching up that shoulder strap,
eager to cinch a tutu round a waist—
even these pathetic attendant monsters
the gods would damn for their smug callousness
and envy for their satin entrances
have claims as firm as ours in this kingdom,
sitting among us in the dark, applauding.

Dance Class

Mothers and aunts squat vigilant on risers:
no man's going to have his way with Sylvie!
Beneath each costume labors one tough cookie—
this one perched on the piano who scratches
her naked back, or that group smoothing tutus,
jinxing the prima ballerina with frosty
stares. The master goads them to mystery—
watch their quick limbs suddenly prove them dancers,
working girls transformed with a single step.
In the mirror, out the window, church spires
or factory chimneys bless the escape
from convent, power loom, or street—these whores
of art, these drudges manufacturing dance
like cloth, these nuns, these brides, these gaslight saints.

Dress Rehearsal

Everyone's so *tired*—one ballerina yawns,
can't stifle it, unless oh God she's screaming,
having lost the black velvet ribbons

she'd felt caressing her waist and neck, dreaming
as she kept pirouetting of their slow
tightening. Her yawn's her penance, damning

the limelight seizing eyes, throat, bodice, elbow
in a silver shimmer, like photography.
Blinded, she wonders where those ribbons go.

Another reaches both hands back to tie
her own ribbon once more round her own throat
while sinking in kind of a sleepy curtsy.

The coryphées look scarcely weary, yet
among the smiles and fluffy tutus one,
fainting, hangs onto a bush—no, not

a bush but a flat painted bushy green,
a sylvan glade from *Sylvia* or *La Fille
Mal Gardée,* the enchanted wood of *Swan*

Lake mimicked by the wood of carpentry.
No, nothing magical's been conjured here,
just sweat, although the prima ballerina

rises on pointe, her arms embracing air,
her attitude, her artifice a denial
of the black-suited men lounging, a leer

winding across their faces like a vile
insinuation. But she's having none
of it, she's in her element, the pull

skyward assumes her, clothed in flesh and satin,
transfiguring exhaustion to pure line
and driving the dance on and on and on.

Serenade

When they waddle into the pizzerias
or the cafés, craving sun-dried tomatoes
and artichoke hearts, you realize they're kids,
babies, whom not so long ago their mothers
swaddled up and shipped off to the city,
gambling the farm on an absurd dream
that ducklings become swans and girls turn dancers.
And here stand seventeen upon the stage,
knockouts made up like nobody's business,
an abstract of blue gowns, their untamed hair
still lush, yet unimprisoned in a chignon,
and look: no longer girls but goddesses,
no longer children wearing baseball caps
and hanging out in restaurants and bars,
lipsticking their ludicrous cigarettes
and rattling like immaculate dice ice cubes
melting like fortune, like an audience.
Now, raising right arms in a gesture of
desire and protest, *Noli me tangere,*
not until they suddenly shift their feet
in unison on a Tschaikovsky chord
do we swear we'd barter our souls or kill
to know the touch of the untouchable,
because those arches, pointed toes, and spaces
glimmering between limbs initiate
a transformation from the merely human
into illusions, into symbols not quite
approachable, not quite warm-blooded—into
dancers. You must know the wonderful story
of Balanchine inventing *Serenade,*
how he made every section for the number
of dancers who showed up at class that day—
he was working with kids, after all, kids
knowing nothing of time, being as gods.
Their puberty and immortality
depended on that first step, that conferral
of divinity by a man who knew,
sometimes, the terrible seductiveness

of restraint, a genius who adored
their teenaged tendons, their thoroughbred limbs,
who understood to set them to Tschaikovsky
would be to set them in the Pantheon.
And when they descend, when they issue through
the stage door, wearing baseball caps no team
has ever worn, and tee shirts of such samite,
so baggy that we study all the harder
the stainless muscles of those sacred arms,
we *want* to feed them, having read of nightmares,
the starving and disgorging, we feel protective
as of a lover waking from the depths,
we need to scent the sacredness of art
because they wreak wild havoc on our glands,
infecting our blood, infiltrating dreams,
plaguing with romantic imbecility
an otherwise sane, fleshly congregation.
No wonder we relax, though startled, to see
them munching on ambrosia, sipping nectar,
seltzer rather, ordering a pizza.

Scenery

Nature bores me so
    it's a relief to find out
        the Romantic landscape
           with its irradiated
                round trees or haystacks, its deep barred shadows,
    and its clouds galloping across the sunset
          is a painted
      backdrop,
             and the boisterous
             verdure of the lush
    shrub lit
    not
    by sunset but
                  by sun
    a painted flat
               one
      dancer uses to prop
      herself up,
               and that the flowers
can bestow
              odors

only of tulle
    and sweat and, faintly, dyes,
    paints, or appliqués,
      since those swatches
    of lilies
      and mums dancing against the painted sunlit bushes
      are, yes, ballet skirts, their hems and stiff stitches
the most unnatural
      thing in the world. I love to watch as
        art
      triumphs, as first one dancer in the wings snatches
          up her shoulder
          strap, then another
    and another, their hair the preposterous
      red of matches,

their rapid steps burning the natural
                                    air
until
        with a tempestuous
                                crescendo in the clear weather
                                it's over
                    and smoothing her floral skirt
        the prima ballerina curtsies
                and clutches
        the brilliant bouquet, flowers
                smacking of dreams, betokening lust, luscious
and unreal.

Rehearsal in Summer

for Kyra Nichols

The *oddness* of attending a rehearsal:
the starts, stops, half-steps, the wobbles off pointe,
the ballet master's abrupt clap to signal
the lagging pianist—it's not yet art,

as though you, all along, were reading rough
drafts of this poem, its grammar wobbly, rhymes
askew, and meter pirouetting off.
But through the stage's mottled chaos gleams

the luminosity of bodies at work:
the prima ballerina's bucktoothed smile,
even in cruel daylight, without make-
up to soften her stark, big-nosed, beguil-

ing homeliness, makes the outdoor stage light up,
then dazzle as this long-legged thoroughbred
bursts into a horselaugh at her missed step
and hitches up her baggy neon sweat-

pants whose faux clumsiness can't disguise
the brilliant rapidity of her limbs.
Her strange patience when her callow cavalier's
not getting it: they try a few more times

that tricky spin where he must catch her at
the last conceivable moment, then they try
again, and yet again in the beastly heat
until finally they look heavenly

in their saturated practice clothes.
But now she stops the pas de deux: the tempo
keeps getting stuck, it's like trying to dance
in mud, or on a stage marleyed with flypaper—

a plunk; a stumble; and now the pianist
at last nails the Tschaikovsky. All at once
the crazyquilt colors of practice clothes
collude kaleidoscopically, the dance

obliterates mere muscle, heavy lifting
translates to flight, and sublime locker room
aromas float off the dancers, wafting
our way to settle on us like perfume.

The Rehearsal Room

In the dark
        rehearsal room
                lit only by
                        dancers
                we can see
                        her dark hair
her bare back
                            not her face.
                Bent fully over
                she adjusts her slipper
                          sole braced
                        against
                a double bass
          carelessly
                left on the floor
      to preside over the gloom;
                out of its somber
bulk
its long neck
              disappears
                            beneath her tulle skirt.
      Watch the bloom
                of skirt on her chair
      transform
                her into a flower
                        a carnation incarnate
                a boutonniere
      hanging on by its stem
                            rehearsing for performance
                        that delicate
              odor
                      in the last light
                        before disappearance
      before the room
goes dark.

Zero Hour

for Debra Fernandez

Uncoiling from dank o-
blivion, an accordion
spreads a rank tango
whose contagious strain

drives dancers to couple
in the marl of shadows:
pulses skitter, nerves ripple
in attraction, bodies

draw heat to heat
in a black back room,
sweat-cleansed, spotlit.
Flirting with vacuum

they drive at a point
to find the point vanished;
the dancers, adamant,
dance on, unvanquished

while their virus infects.
Oh pestilent tango
inexorable as sex,
rush us to zero.

Blue Dancers

The merest line of black paint holds in check
the blue contagion of their ballet skirts,
a haze toxic as blue chlorine, that starts
in dancers' glands and, blooming like siren smoke
from backstage, would overcome us and infect
our lungs with sky-bright grief. One dancer parts
unruly hair, another fondles her arch,
preparing us for mindlessness, the wreck
we choose over our tidy lives, transported
to realms bolted on feathery illusions.
Steel-boned, murderous sylphs, gossamer-skirted,
they render us light-lunged, hollow-hearted.
Breathe their smudgy bodies' emanations,
lap their brushstrokes' poisonous emulsions.

Adagio

Slowing, the oboe swoons in the orchestral
swell: if a girl denoting six o'clock,
thrusting one leg behind her toward the sky
were not enough to make us gasp, that leg
imparts momentum to her head's downstroke
so her forehead touches her other knee,
all this on pointe—enough to make you fall
in love a hundred-fifty feet away.
I loved a dancer once, and watching her
do that with her body in front of two
thousand people I suddenly couldn't breathe
until she'd lift her head once more and lower
that leg I knew, and send me on toward death—
that firm, amazing leg, those years ago.

Mid-Air

A dance that ends in mid-air doesn't end.
The stage blacks out, but there's no curtain call,
for even if the curtain should descend

the dancers, turned to shadows, still extend
their breathless steps behind the fabric wall.
The dance that ends in mid-air cannot end

for Orpheus, bound for a distant land
bearing his torch into the lightless hall,
where even if the curtain should descend,

eye losing eye, hand suddenly seeking hand,
the glancing blow of tragedy won't stall
the dance that ends mid-air: it cannot end

all gravity, the dancers' upright friend
who sets them leaping, keeping us in thrall.
Then even if the curtain should descend

on our performance, looking back we send
our bodies forward, leaping to a fall—
a dance that ends mid-air and doesn't end,
not even when the curtain must descend.

Valedictorian

We all broke out, all ached, but I remember
the senior prom, his geometric pace
around and around the gym floor, his eyes
unswerving from its painted black perimeter.
If I made up a name like Samson Gruber—
but Christ, I can't: it's too ridiculous.
Inside a head mopped with a blond thunder-
storm, lightning danced, blazing with calculus,
waltzing him into a world of forms. Princeton
opened opulent arms to him that fall;
he scaled the summit, clambering to the top
of the math building. One calculated step
perfect as a pinpoint, and he danced on
air, elegant and breathless as an angel.

Chaconne

In the chaconne the steps are elegant.
The couple walk like gods, almost fallen,
in fragile majesty. Their arms extend
permitting her sweep near the ground, her orbit
justified by gravity, her planet
granting them momentum, an illusion
of love, no sign of flaring out or strain:
their exit keeps a courtship's perfect secret.
In the music's serene agony live
death and mourning, the end of the end:
eye loses eye and hand releases hand.
Of all things bearing scrutiny, love
bears least, the barest look forcing its flight,
the solemn logic of a sorrowing flute.

The Oceana Roll

Chaplin, *The Gold Rush*

So picking up two forks
you stab two dinner rolls.
The women swoon at the rolls' high kicks.
Round, with flattened soles

like your own stupid shoes,
they adorably execute
ronds de jambe and entrechats,
landing in a split.

You make chaste little bows,
and the bread rolls shuffle off.
Your best girl claims a luxurious kiss,
knocking you cold and stiff.

Later you'll wake to find
your goose cooked black and cold, candles
shrunk, gifts still wrapped—you've wined and dined
no one. Your mind meanders

back to all those parties
you imagined, carryings on
in loud, naughty ballrooms, soirées
by private invitation

where all behaved unspeakably,
the eighth-grade femme fatale
stopping boy after boy
with hard lips and mouth full

of tongue, or the cheerleader
extruding a moan
with her touch. But now you're the center
of all girlish attention,

all the ones who've snubbed you
since kindergarten
who should have known, who should have loved you,
now applauding *Darling*

with fluttering lashes.
Wind and animals howl
outside in the Yukon. Blind snow surges.
Speech! the women call,

Speech! Silence from your smile;
a title card tells all:
Ladies, I am speechless! But I will
perform the Oceana Roll.

Exuberance

for Sigrid Nunez

Drunk of course, so we were dancing up
the proverbial storm in our hosts' living room,
cutting a Persian rug. I caught you in my arm
and swung you round one, then the other hip;
then, back to back, I launched you in a flip
overhead. You kicked their Tiffany museum
piece, the chandelier. In the tomblike hush—our tomb—
it swung wild, slowing to a heart-stopped stop.
Nights passed like that in our exuberance,
lit from within with a bright stupid grace
that wouldn't last—our high-stepping destroying
other fixtures, stained shards glittering
like jewels. Barefoot, reeling on smashed glass,
no wonder we overthrew the bloody dance.

The Lesson of Orpheus

You play blind. She depends
        on you, her dead legs
trailing in your dance.
You advance
                by echolocation,
                        chords plucked from gut-strings
                like light raptured from the sun
        into the gloom. She drags
                you down
        one step for every two you rise, and tugs
                        at your shoulders where she clings
                like exquisite stone
                        wings.
                        She longs

to twine
around you like a vine
        to crawl
all the long way up from underground.
                She demands you see her,
                        embrace her flesh bruised like fruit,
                        claim the clammy papyrus of the winding sheet,
                the hiss in your ear,
        the keen perfume in your nostril.
                Sheathed in the sound armor
                of your lyre
                                you ravel out music
                                to trick
your veneration
                into desire.

Who has not tried to revive
a dead love?
        Dance floors,
                dinners spiked with wine
        and regret, hours

silent, supine,
        uncoiled on sofas, hand
        chilling in hand.
        The papers all but signed,
        we went out dancing, a kind
        of celebration. My hand

massaged the muscles of her back,
        those twin embankments either side
                of the forgetful river,
its undulating current a swift shock.
        A sigh, the dead
        weight of her head
                on my shoulder:
I could get her back.
Flick:
        my eyes opened: I made her
        disappear.

Navigating her through Hades'
        lips back into life,
        braille hand reading her chest for breath,
                her nipples
        for a word, heart stiffened for stillbirth,
you dance close
to the surface,
        rumpling the crust like moles,
                near-
                ly breathing air,
faint music through the humus,
        a lilt in the loam, the beautiful filth
                you'll never scour out from under
        her nails.
        A bird warbles
        diminished scales,
                her joints' percussion

                    knocking nearer
                            and you turn, you always turn
        to see her iris

                            spiral shut, the dawn
                fold its petals

                            into stone.

Translated

Crowned
      with an ass's head you get to partner
            the queen, the queen
            of fairies, the queen
            of the company. Stumbling as in a swoon,
                as if you've lost your glasses,
      you're bewildered how this creature
                  with her ethereal
                  limbs and unimaginable
            crevices
extends to you beyond
            the reach of vision
      her gossamer
            softnesses
            veiling your eyes
            ludicrous with happiness.

Yet you partner beautifully,
      your braying and tentative trotting
somehow supporting her in the pas de deux,
      responding
            to moonlit promise,
      handling
her sleek calf and royal thigh.
      It's everything
              I dream of, someone
                to scratch
      my ears and admire their hairs sprouting
              and in devotion
      tender my wise
                age
            parted lips, open
      limbs. Open eyes.

Dance of the Snowflakes

I have never paid the weather
enough mind never
      taken the year's turnings
      as intimations or longings
            of any but my own and not some human
            global or cosmic condition

so it's time to dance
attendance
      on the snow not the snow
          we shove out
      of the driveway and the plow
          plows back in not
the creaking shushing snow breaking the liquid silence
          beneath my skis but

the breathtaking white body
      we can apprehend
          if we care to its crystal
          glint and shimmer its structural
          miracle
      its ability to suspend
our intellectual pertinacity

so the revelation *it's snowing*
      descends with accumulations
      of flutes and violins
          in an insistent
             swirl
             a circular
          flurry whose silent
concealing
          uncovers an elegant
            structure
this white body tempting the hands

because the snow as it piles up acquires
      density and heft

though that's not what I'm after here
rather
the illusion that, falling, it's soft
that it's living and passionate that it coheres
that as it snugs and embraces this world we imagine ours
it cares

about us the way we fantasize
those dancers
flurrying onstage to Tschaikovsky's
music care, skittering, gliding
singly
then collectively
snow flying from the flies
no sign
of the storm stopping
a squall of tutus
a body of dancers
a corps of course, the ballet's
crystalline
intricacies

visible from heaven
the fourth ring
without magnification
how the tulle and satin
and flesh of the human
women
whose implicit joy and desire now burst mysteriously
into song
collect in a mathematically
intricate and moving

corporeal
mass
aromas
arising from their sweating and scented
bodies

to travel
        I imagine heavenward

yet each one on pointe unique
        in the construction of her hands
        in the instructions of her genes
unique unique
          in her eyes and lips
            in her fingernails
        her steps
          following those of everyone else

unique

as each snow-
       flake
         beyond its six-
         pointed generics
           on pointe
and each toe-
          shoe a point
      points engendering an oblique
        angle its vertex
            a fine place to start
            isn't it
     a vortex
              a good end
               a human shelter
               from weather
    this genetic
                 flurry
           these emerging imagined
white limbs of snow
        embracing, enfolding, each one different
              melting me.

The House

The house is packed, stacked. Bodies assemble
to watch a ballerina in a hush
of music—make it Suzanne Farrell—push
sex skyward into an ethereal
realm. Here in the fourth balcony hearts tremble
at such elevation, her arabesque
rippling up through the dark while ushers blush
at the elongate angle of her ankle.
The Gothic architecture of her body
obliterates all sense of ours, its lame
excuses melting with its aches. My lady
is built like that, propped up by knees and elbows;
the shelter of her hair, her hearth call, "Dance."
Enter, and be danced to another home.

Making a Fool of Myself over Maria Kowroski

Streamlined as the ornament on a Packard,
swan in takeoff under the ghostly blue stage
light, her face a sphinxlike, impassive icon
      chocked with Tschaikovsky,

she's a dancer Balanchine would have loved, loved
bone and sinew, heir to the muse's mantle,
lunar-cruel and stupid with genius: music,
      movement, and blank sex

knocking not the crotch but my chest and poor brain.
Charming? More like paralyzed: eyes gone flashbulbs,
air turned flame and raptured from lungs, my glib tongue
      dumbing to granite.

Later, wrecked, I'm meeting her face to face, her
twenty-two exquisitely unabashed years
smiling through some party our town has thrown these
      dancerly creatures,

cheese, champagne, some boxes of Girl Scout cookies.
Glass in hand, "Maria Kowroski?" I say,
"You—your dancing—'thrilling's' the only word. I
      sit in the dark, thrilled."

Smiling, she is cooing, "How sweet!" but no—it's
hell, not sweet—I want her to know I'm kept up
nights to partner succubus limbs that burn the
      phosphorus air, so

quick they torch the dreck out of human passion,
moonlit arms abandoning me to darkness.
Now her smile is faltering, now my wife says,
      "Don't be afraid, he

gets this way sometimes, but he's harmless, really."
God, I've bought a pair of your satin toe shoes,

battered, hardened, stripped of their ribbons, nude pink,
      ragged with pointework,

shoes your feet have danced in, where sweat-conducted
contacts sparked to generate light, divine toes
crammed in boxes signed by your hand. My hands now
      fondling your footsteps,

hear me out, Terpsichore, on my kneebones:
drive me crazy, cripple my days with beauty;
naked relics clutched to my cheek, I breathe their
      reek of sheer ether.

Sonnambula

for Darci Kistler

What a party! brocaded ladies,
their bodices flirtatious
        as armor,
            the air exploding
                in sequins and thick
as narcissus
        liquor—
                      what
slender promise
                for the poet!
morose,
           romantic,
        believing

in nothing
        not even it seems
           poetry—
                when down
                from a garret, a tower, down
           among the jeweled finery
                down
        from dreams
           wearing nearly
nothing,
                a nightgown,
                a shift, down
        from asylum
                she lights, candle-laden
among the living.

No breath
        stirs her flame
           that even the wind can't extinguish,
        yet it is flame,
           it would singe,

it would translate helpless to do otherwise a moth
                    to ash.
                                If you turned
                                        her gently
                                        by her visionary
                        hand,
                                    she'd spin on pointe endlessly
                        almost. If you twined
                                        in her limbs and pressed
                                        against
                        her nightgowned
                                body
                                if this could be a body
                        and not an apparition,
                                        a ghost,
            if this were no dream—

The hazard
        of this occupation,
                this precarious
                        craft! In the teeth
            of the evidence
I'd
        commit to her, this nightgown,
                this slip, this sylph
                        in her unnatural
                strength
                worth . . .
                        well,
            to dance like that! like no one!
I'd
be carried
                                        by her
                effortless-
                                        ly up her tower
up over the jeweled
gaping crowd,

                                        the poet

committed,
                              a glimmer in the air,
                              a flicker
                                        in the

night:
                    farewell.

2   *Danses Macabres*

Every description of lascivious motion, every gesture that is offensive to modesty, and whatever can corrupt innocence and honesty is represented by these dancers, to the life. Alternately do they salute, exchanging amorous looks; they give to their hips a certain immodest motion, then they meet and press their breasts together; their eyes appear half closed, and they seem, even while dancing, to be approaching the final embrace.

    —Carlo Blasis, *The Code of Terpsichore* (1828)

Cold is better.

    —George Balanchine

i.

Death Goes to a Party

Death does the hokey pokey and he turns
himself around. Music makes you believe
hair grows on scalpless skulls and bare bones jive:
look at those party-animal skeletons,
piles of knuckles, pothooks, and plumbers' joints
reveling naked. They've got to grin, they wave
to a corpse tumbling in an open grave
with worms bopping about its sunshine bones.
Thus concludes the history of the world,
no whimpering but a great rowdy shout,
a clatter and crash like crockery, pots hurled
about the kitchen, hipbones shaking it
in and out, all bones set on making it
one last smashing time. That's what it's all about.

Death's Comfort

It comforts me, Death's flat-out impotence
can never stimulate the limp to rise—
tempting and cold, level as wilderness,
unleavened as wafer-bread. Who wants
dead darlings to suffer resurrections?
Elbow grease could not stop Lazarus
from stinking, nor desire help Orpheus
from flinging Eurydice a backward glance.
All art aims to flesh out how we reject
the dead. Yet here Death stands, flush as gangrene
with lust, his skin dripping in putrefaction.
He has designs. He plans to dance erect
behind her and seal her purification
with his John Hancock on her ghost-white skin.

Death's Move

His *modus* is to sneak up from behind,
fingers first on her shoulder, then her supple
waist, wasting little time, sciatic ripple
rung down her thigh, breath hissing from beyond
he loves her for her body, fuck her mind;
insinuating thumb dinging her nipple,
his bone-hand grasps her saucy breast, an apple
whose sleek skin trembles at his scaly rind.
His grin gapes in a tattered mask of scarlets
like torn wallpaper; ragged muscle lines
his hands like ghastly orchard gloves. She starts,
then darting her hand downward she disheartens
or spurs on his stalking fingerbones,
those prunehooks angling underneath her skirts.

Death in Waiting

Shucking the body, he says, is no harder,
no more painful than a contorted dance,
like wriggling out of skintight cocktail gowns,
first the dizzying glimpse of luminous shoulder,
wave action next, the hot unzip and slither:
breasts inspire gasps and belly stiffens,
then over the hips and out, the emergence
into chilled air rendering all things harder.
And he stands watching, waiting to assist,
eager to expose, he says, the best
in us all, the permanent thing, whose clean
lines and eloquent articulation
seduce our future into a loving past
as brilliant, hard, and stupid as the moon.

Death's Deal

What a joker, that Death, what a card.
We tell him, *Have a heart,* and so he steals
ours, the shyster, steals our parents', our girl's.
He can lay it on with a trowel, a spade,
dig? He does, and he bops us on the mazzard,
we're playing with an empty deck. He deals
an arsenal of clubs, heartless black coals
for diamonds, kings committing suicide.
Then scooping up his chips, without ado
he's off, and you can breathe. You've saved your skin,
you've kept your shirt; then the bell tolls. The phone,
he's calling from booth 13, he's got a bone
to pick, he's got your number, he wants to chew
the fat. And he's got such a deal for you.

Death Contemplates the Resurrection of Capital Punishment

Deterrent? What deterrent? He knows murder
rates won't plummet. Those ghouls in politics—
what pimps! Polls soar when Death smokes hot as sex:
he gets two stiffs for one. It's a no-brainer!
He wishes they'd revive the draw-and-quarter,
the guillotine. That tidy gurney looks
about as thrilling as when the vet injects
your dog. My friends, a killer's not a hamster.
No! give him those old-time electrocutions—
great choreography, blew away the noose,
the zany ways that chair got folks to dance.
Plug in, switch on, and dig those bugging eyes,
those socket-popping spheres, and treat your nose
to frying meat, to crap shot in the pants.

Death's Door

His entrance freeze-dries everything. Tears harden
to pearls, streaming hair chills to marble sculpture.
The fleeing body halts, a salty pillar,
its hysterical, flailing limbs sublimed to bone
china, a ghost swastika. Old Death has gone
quite stiff himself; he finds it's gotten harder
to tussle schoolgirls surprised on the stair
and keep those assignations in the garden.
It's such a rigorous, demanding schedule
he'll make his ribs a door and keep it locked
on his stiff heart, two peepholes in his skull.
Then salesmen, wives, Jehovah's Witnesses,
and Girl Scouts offering their timid cookies
can let him taste their wares and buy direct.

Death and the 7-Year-Old Pilot

An ice-dancing propeller, a waggling wing,
and this precocious kid, sights set on stars,
has flown beyond congratulatory wires,
her spoiled, daredevil birthday lust for flying
having smacked her with a pancake landing.
Cloud-frosting, lamppost-candles, homes and cars
swooped up at her, and then the cake was hers,
the whole world in her hands, fiery earthling,
poor budding pilot. Death the pederast
owns no trousers to keep it in, no closet
to pop out of, unlike us: we'll beg,
steal for these secure wardrobes, arm and a leg
maintenance, while in pink rooms, in secret
mirrors, our girls waltz, preening for their tryst.

Sweet Decorum

for Sarah Webster Goodwin

One fiery breath and down like dominoes
they tumble. Death's triumph, the Great War: ranks
of boys rising like zombies from the trench
to dance in No Man's Land. Machine guns hose
them, spattering the earth so little grows
despite the plowing underground by tanks,
despite lifeblood and fertilizer. In France
white crosses bloom for miles. Demure in rows,
scrubbed as schoolchildren in uniform lines,
like girls not yet menstruating, unkissed
they lie. We lie to say they lie asleep,
a sweet nap after a sapping field trip,
as if they'll wake to milk and macaroons,
their carved names saving them from getting lost.

Matter of Death

Ambrosia, angel food cake, that's how sweet
Death's excrement should logically tang,
victoriously hurled out with no sting,
maybe a tingle tart as pomegranate
seeds, clitoral, resilient, radiant light
escaping. We rescue jewels from dirt, loving
the way anatomy attracts the tongue
to honey, plunging the nose in the pit.
Dante once wriggled blindly up Hell's sphincter,
buggering the final mineshaft, that center
of Gravity. He rhymed—after his exit—
its brilliant voidings: the heavenly starlit
dome. Light can't hold a candle to dark matter,
which outweighs all we see. Death's shit is shit.

First Dance

Flaming angels their only chaperones,
no nosy parents: they could please themselves.
But browsing through the golden record shelves
they couldn't pick the consummate first dance
for treading the ground in time, a song that *ends*—
no choirs, no heads of pins—a dance for dives
and big exits. Now they stumbled, their calves
sore with work, out of practice on their spins,
hopeless on dips. *We've Only Just Begun?*
In Eden, even *Build Me Up Buttercup*
smacked of nectar. Out here, no *Satisfaction,*
no rebirth; more like a resurrection
into new-bruised bodies. *Pick yourself up,*
dust yourself off, start all over again.

ii.

Horoscope

for Joseph Caldwell

Go out dancing and you may break your neck.
Show others your keen and morbid sense of humor.
Highfalutin theories sound great, but rumor
has it you will come down to earth. At work
enthusiasm will infect you. Check
your physical woes and your health at the door:
family could be impressed by a tumor.
Purchase a plot of real estate for luck.
Mention what you want, and you won't get it.
Paranormal abilities may surface.
Reward children with praise and legacies.
Let love stab you in the back. Start a riot.
Confuse the issues. Lose hope. Be concise.
Stop all this nonsense. Lie down and be quiet.

Death and the Maiden

He's struck up a lively tarantella to un-
lock the darkening mirror from her hand
and spider to smithereens the skull that grinned
back baldfaced in longing and rude reflection.
The *moto perpetuo* of his machine
he keeps well oiled: he'll mire her in the mud,
his variations conveying her round and round,
at last conducting her in a straight line
downward. Now his scherzo stirs her to waltz
stiffly, till her prim self-consciousness melts
and she's a virgin dancing like a flame—
snuffed to nothing as all movement dwindles
to his elemental theme. Not wine, not candles,
not his stirring coda can make her warm.

Death Makes the Man

Cue lightning to flash, cue thunder to pound
against the cellar window while he stitches
some last embroidery. Now he attaches
the electrodes—but before the resurrection
he stands back to admire his manly hand-
iwork: the polished bolts, the zillion switches
that flip the nervous system, the jeweled crotch's
artful setting. Yes, topnotch skin and bone,
quality parts, for he recalls his younger
cock-ups, that Hollywood job that still lumbers
flatfooted like a hippo through his nightmares.
He needs a dreamboat, not a Schwarzenegger,
something to lure the young girls from their chambers
for dirty dancing, a member that remembers.

Death's Sentence

Even the guard whistling *Für Elise*
bears him a kind of grudging admiration
and, passing, stops dopplering his baton
down the cell row's ribs, where the great prince, Death, lies
in prison, lies on his bunk dreaming, lies
to homeboys, gangbangers, to anyone
who'll listen how women, men, pretty children
requited his love, how they swapped their lives
for meaningful abstraction, how they adored
his extremities' probing, his profound love-
play stopping ears, mouths, throats, and orifices
more occult, how he'll sweet-talk the Board, news
to scream through the neighborhood when he's off
Death Row and on parole, good as his word.

Death the Dietician

She won't eat, she can't eat, but that's okay,
she must impersonate a rail to dance,
she must maintain her cold line in performance.
Potato chip or two, try to choke
a cup of yogurt down, a Diet Coke
say, every other day. He calms the parents:
it's good to see them dancing in their bones,
the scrawniest, the unripe—those he'll pluck.
He's got this thing, see, less for little girls
than women slamming the brakes on being women.
He gets off on the flat chest, on the prison
of a stark ribcage, on the annihilation
of the bloody cycle. It's no curse,
fruitlessness. That apple he munches was hers.

Death's Theater

It's not all tragedy; he's not averse
to melodrama if everyone gets shot,
or musical comedy if the plot
is big and earthy, with a crop of chorus
girls good enough to eat. He loves a farce,
that nervous frenzy, those doors slamming shut
in your face. He's Mr. Opening Night,
top hat and cape, arriving in a hearse,
knocking them dead, each show a limited run:
one performance, curtain up, curtain down.
He'll undertake conning supporting roles,
rebuild the sets, rewrite your lines. He peddles
tickets, and pens reviews in which you shine.
He sends flowers. He coughs through your big scene.

Death's Addiction

Death inspires you and fingers every stop,
tickling your holes with whistling breath, his hot
wind playing your bones like an Aeolian lute.
And in his embouchure's embrace, at his lip
like a cigarette, you inspire him: each deep
drag sucking forth your soul can illuminate
nothing but itself, a red warning light
filtering you to ash, down to the tip
of his finger. You are his cancer, you fill
his lungs with the luminous holes he thrives
on, and drawing you out he scans the bar
for the next sucker who desperately craves
his cure. Grinding your butt under his heel
he lights one up and takes her to the floor.

Black Angels Play *Death and the Maiden*

The house is dead tonight. No one forgives
this performance. They should barely be touching
the strings, delicately as tendons hushing
against bone, like a gasp, like vanished loves
playing peek-a-boo under fallen leaves.
But the cello growls, the violin starts screeching,
then strokes so hard the guts rebel, retching,
the barked notes scurrying from their dry heaves.
They scrape a dead pavane above their fingers
where the guts scroll back into their instruments;
on crystal goblets they bow broken hints
of wheezing gongs invoking ancient hungers,
dry crumbs of planetary sarabandes
leaving absence, an odor—fear—that lingers.

Death's Animation

Shot out of an inkwell in the Fleischer
Studios, Death tapdanced in jazz cartoons,
fronting a corps of corpses, skeletons
and Betty Boop—a *ree*-al hoochie-coocher,
sweet Betty, rolling cow eyes as her jitter-
bugging garters sparked like séance hands,
inspiring ghosts to ectoplasmic dance,
knocking joints into an upright posture,
a future cocked of animated bones.
Filmgoers flipped at headless resurrections—
such a gas that *hi-de-hi-de-hi-de-hi*
a star was born, *boop-boop-be-doop*. Far away
in Europe ink fled back to the black bottle
for soon bones wouldn't dance, or rise at all.

Death Sings Lieder

for Tom Denny

He's a poet, Death's a goddamn poet,
Romantic but nobody's fool, a tear-
jerking good read, sucker of sap, extruder
of juice. The young maid fears she's going to get it.
Oh where, oh where's his heart? She sees right through it,
she screams *Don't do it,* she wails *Oy vey iz mir!*
Reading her fevered lips, he translates fear
into *Darling,* crooned in Ultraviolet.
Singing her delicate and beautiful,
Death gets under her skin, where he'll tease out
what shines in her. His hand will stroke, not slap:
he'll make her purr, not prey, tame as any cat.
By the time he rings his final rhyme, she'll sleep
soundlessly, head hard on his clavicle.

La Valse

Only Death can keep commitments: girls flirt
and withdraw, flirt and withdraw, the music
consumptive, languishing as lust grows sick
and dies. Wallflowers! One fluffs and smooths her skirt,
and with her white-gloved hand she masks her heart,
then her face, until he sweeps in to take
her in his arms like an electric shock
while the waltz threatens to blow itself apart,
thundering, screaming. Dyeing her ballgown black,
he offers her a mirror where she can read
no reflection, the glass cracked and opaque.
She lets him gather her, waltzing, and freed
from time, she's raised dead-center. Around
her race the idiot dancers, hand-in-hand.

iii.

Last Dance

Fifties sock hops mortified us, necros
in death-embraces, the teen dreck we listened
to morbid as puberty. When they found
you in his arms, my girl, America's
girl, high school ring clutched tightly in his knuckles,
its 7-Up bottle-glass emerald ground
to dust, your T-Bird's radio still moaned.
Your car's shards had divorced us, sure as sickles
cutting grain. We could never dance to it;
his last kiss would linger on blood-red lips
I never got to smear. Now, heavenly
shades swooning with your rapture, thunderclaps
for bass drums, it's number one with a bullet.
Darling, he sings, *save the last dance for me.*

Death's Sympathy

He felt bad for them—not guilty, just bad
enough to offer them some stately twangling
on his ukulele as they left, straggling
as in a funeral dance. He'd play their guide,
helping them choose their rest stops while they cried
tears, naturally; he'd boost their pride, rankling
with rejection; he'd help the poor guy drudging—
he'd shovel, jawboning side by side, same side
his wife sprang from, supermodel-gaunt, bone-
thin then, now *zaftig,* apple-cheeked, windfall-
fed. But their endless busy-work! Toil, spin,
each day wasted in digging a deeper hole—
for what? Let her keep cooing at their son
nursing, the one he'd heard them call, yes, Cain.

Death's Love

I saw an old man hobble down the street
on the arm of his grown grandson. It touched
me, those generations linked, his claw hooked
on that arm, that stride helping his shambling gait.
Then his eyes probed me from a sunken pit,
young, positive as new blue stars. That spooked
me, smooth skin stretched over the skull. I looked
at window dressing till they'd passed, then sat
sucking ice cubes chuckling in a tall drink.
Grow old along with me. Could I live marriage
in real time while mad acceleration
sped my darling toward light? Our skeleton
masks hide skeletons, so it's no joke
how Death loves us and molds us in his image.

Death in Disguise

By no means young, but she was not old either.
Like rain I recall the afternoon her songs
first swerved baldly off key. The clockwork springs
of my childhood went *ka-boing;* I cried. Mother
by the end wore her body like a sweater
shrunk comically too tight, like Death in paintings
with skin the tarpaulin color of tarred lungs,
a master of disguise dolled up as cancer,
the true comedian as the letter C:
twining himself round any alphabet
as subtly as snaking through a tree,
he steals away our speech, leaving us deaf,
dumb, screaming we must shuck love, regret
life. Comedian? More like the letter F.

Death's Portrait

for Frances Cohen Gillespie

Nothing like lead white to keep you young.
He dabs it on to highlight sexy flesh
and intimate how diligently he'll bleach
the whiteness underneath that all along
has posed patiently for him. He'll hang
you in the cellar. Dust will fuzz your varnish,
your bloom will flake away, your eyes' light vanish,
lush hair go cobweb, all those vain hours sitting—
wasted. But nothing's permanent. Today's
safe media and colors prove poisonous
tomorrow. Gorgeous toxins penetrate
his subjects, but he'll protect his investment,
stripping your glazes one by one to restore
his own face underpainted in your mirror.

Death the Mother

Stevens nailed it: Death is the mother of Beauty.
I know, since Beauty endlessly would bitch
about each bruise, about the jealous watch
her mother kept. Like twins they looked, uncanny
as mother-daughter douche commercials. Tasty
all tarted up, mom couldn't act her age,
embalmed in heavy scent, flaunting a bonus flash
of flesh, that black lipstick. Beauty would cry,
cursing her mom for teaching her the dance
that she, by nature, couldn't help but lead.
She brought me home, and it still thrills and sickens
me how her deep-voiced, long-legged mama, clad
in Beauty's lace bra, cocktail frock, black stockings,
lay in wait all night to jump my bones.

Death in the Woods

My wavery window glass makes it appear
something out there's moving among the trees,
out where the woodchuck nibbles at the grass,
out where the raccoon feels that rabid whirr
like a lawnmower savage his nerves' core.
As I shift my weight behind the glass,
tree bends to tree, unhelped by any breeze.
I hear them whisper, and I know conspir-
acies green with chlorophyll are afoot:
he's sprouted leaves for manufacturing
his own dark sustenance; his parasite root
nurses at the breast of my decomposing
mother, and his blossoms broadcast spring
to hide the preparation of his fruit.

Reception

What had that wedding dress to do with white?
For you were something borrowed, something blue,
shrouded in eyelet, white skin shining through
like moth-holes in a lampshade, and I dreamt
how later that night you would radiate
a love-glow like a bug-light's indigo,
as luminous as chemotherapy.
Who'd guess you'd planned to disappear? As night
dropped its veil I surprised you in the barn
grinding your hips against one of the ushers
I didn't recognize, an old friend of yours.
The bone-web of his hand kneaded your luscious
buttocks, sawdust soaked up your bridal stain;
you pressed lips on teeth, dancing flesh to bone.

Breathless

for Hilary Sio

I dreamed I brought you back from underground
and for a time in time I repossessed
your breathless self, whom gravely I undressed.
Your stocking's black whisper under my hand,
your black garter's stutter against blood-drained,
squid-white flesh, the ultimate minimalist
art, despite your time passed away, amazed
me with arousal. We danced again, we sinned
as if there were no tomorrow. Each tear
that sprang abrupt and human to your eyes
sparkled and said I dreamed. You weren't there
after all these damned years: ever faithless,
the party girl, sucker for a black leather
jacket, ever the dirty adulteress.

Death at Midnight

We knew it would be touch and go. My songs
proved fruitless. They caressed you in the cradle
but you left anyway. At night I still
hear distant dancing music, the plucked strings,
the clucking of the bones: on flapping wings
he drops in to adopt you, kiss you, snuggle
you, then climb dark air as on a bicycle
while night wind rushing through his bone-spokes sings.
My babe so beautiful! it chills my heart
with terror just to look upon your stone.
I see you dancing naked in some Death-
run nightcare center, a blueblood spoiled from birth,
instead of planted in the pristine dirt
where you have not and never can be grown.

Curtain Call

The ballet master tendered his gaunt hand
and made you immortal. I'd never seen
your eyes so dark, skin so pale, legs so open
to choreography; your suave new friend,
not I, would partner those fine bones in the end.
Phantasmal, Pavlova dancing the dawn,
rising elusive as a dying swan,
your steps echoing in a distant land,
for years you dazzled him; his company
grew desolate without you. As you dance
away, I'm left with smoke and intermissions.
Linger among us longer than customary
for a last curtsy, *la grande révérence,*
clutching fall flowers before blood-red curtains.

Come Away, Death

Now, at last, I've grown sick and tired of Death,
his filthy lust, his holocausts, his craving
for martyr-bombs and subway gas, his dancing
in vile denial like a psychopath,
his upbraiding my loved ones in the earth.
Grief's time-consuming and hardly beats living.
I won't dance. That stopped when I watched my darling
strike her last attitude, bereft of breath.
The pen she left me just dropped to the floor,
staining our red rug black with ink. A car
door slams, late-year Mercedes, triple-black.
Who's got my shoes? A hammering at the door.
Bang goes my alarm clock. Time to stop work.

Acknowledgments

MANY THANKS TO the editors of journals where most of these poems originally appeared, sometimes in different form: *American Literary Review:* "Dress Rehearsal"; *Beloit Poetry Journal:* "Latin Class"; *Chautauqua Literary Review:* "Dance Class"; *Chelsea:* "Breathless," "Come Away, Death," "Death at Midnight," "Death in Disguise," and "Reception"; *Comstock Review:* "Death in Waiting"; *Confrontation:* "Turnout" (as "Turned Out"); *Crazyhorse:* "Valedictorian"; *Georgia Review:* "Rehearsal in Summer"; *Green Mountains Review:* "Blue Dancers," "First Dance," "Last Dance," and "Yellow Dancers"; *Grove Review:* "Death's Addiction"; *Hopkins Review:* "Adagio"; *Hotel Amerika:* "Death's Animation"; *Kenyon Review:* "Dance of the Snowflakes," "Museum," and "The Rehearsal Room"; *Literary Imagination:* "Exuberance," "The House," and "Making a Fool of Myself over Maria Kowroski"; *Many Mountains Moving:* "Scenery"; *Margie:* "Death and the 7-Year-Old Pilot"; *Marlboro Review:* "Death in the Woods" and "Death Makes the Man"; *Nimrod:* "Death Goes to a Party" and "Death's Sympathy"; *North American Review:* "Death's Move" and "Zero Hour"; *Notre Dame Review:* "Death and the Maiden," "Death's Comfort," "Death's Door," "Death's Sentence," and "Death Sings Lieder"; *Paper Street:* "Sweet Decorum"; *Prairie Schooner:* "Death's Portrait"; *Quarterly West:* "Primavera"; *Salmagundi:* "Degas's Men" and "Invocation"; *Sewanee Review:* "Black Angels Play Death and the Maiden," "Curtain Call," "Death's Theater," and "La Valse"; *Southern Review:* "Chaconne," "Death Contemplates the Resurrection of Capital Punishment," and "Translated"; *Southwest Review:* "Mid-Air" and "Serenade"; *Texas Review:* "Horoscope" and "The Oceana Roll"; *Visions-International:* "Death's Deal" and "Death the Dietician"; *Western Humanities Review:* "Umbrella Pines"; *Witness:* "Death's Love."

"Sonnambula" appeared in souvenir programs for two celebrations of New York City Ballet principal dancer Darci Kistler in Saratoga Springs, New York: the Saratoga Performing Arts Center Ballet Gala, 11 July 2009, and the National Museum of Dance Darci Kistler Tribute, 17 July 2009.

A selection of the "Danses Macabres" sequence appeared as a letterpress chapbook, *Twenty Danses Macabres,* published in 2010 by Spring Garden Press as winner of the 2009 Robert Watson Poetry Award.

"Invocation," "Rehearsal in Summer," "Serenade," and "Translated" were reprinted in *Ballet Beat;* "Museum" in *Lake George Arts Project Literary Review;* and "Degas's Men" and "Invocation" in *The Second Word Thursdays Anthology.*

I am most grateful to the Corporation of Yaddo for residencies during which I worked on many of these poems. I also thank the Faculty Development Committee of Skidmore College for its generous support.

For their advice and encouragement, I owe thanks to Terry Diggory, Siobhan Dunham, John Easterly, Debra Fernandez, Andrew Hudgins, Sigrid Nunez, Elizabeth Zimmer, and, above all, Penny Jolly.

www.ingramcontent.com/pod-product-compliance
Lightning Source LLC
Chambersburg PA
CBHW031523270326
41930CB00006B/494